AF898622

SUPER SHARKS

BULL SHARK

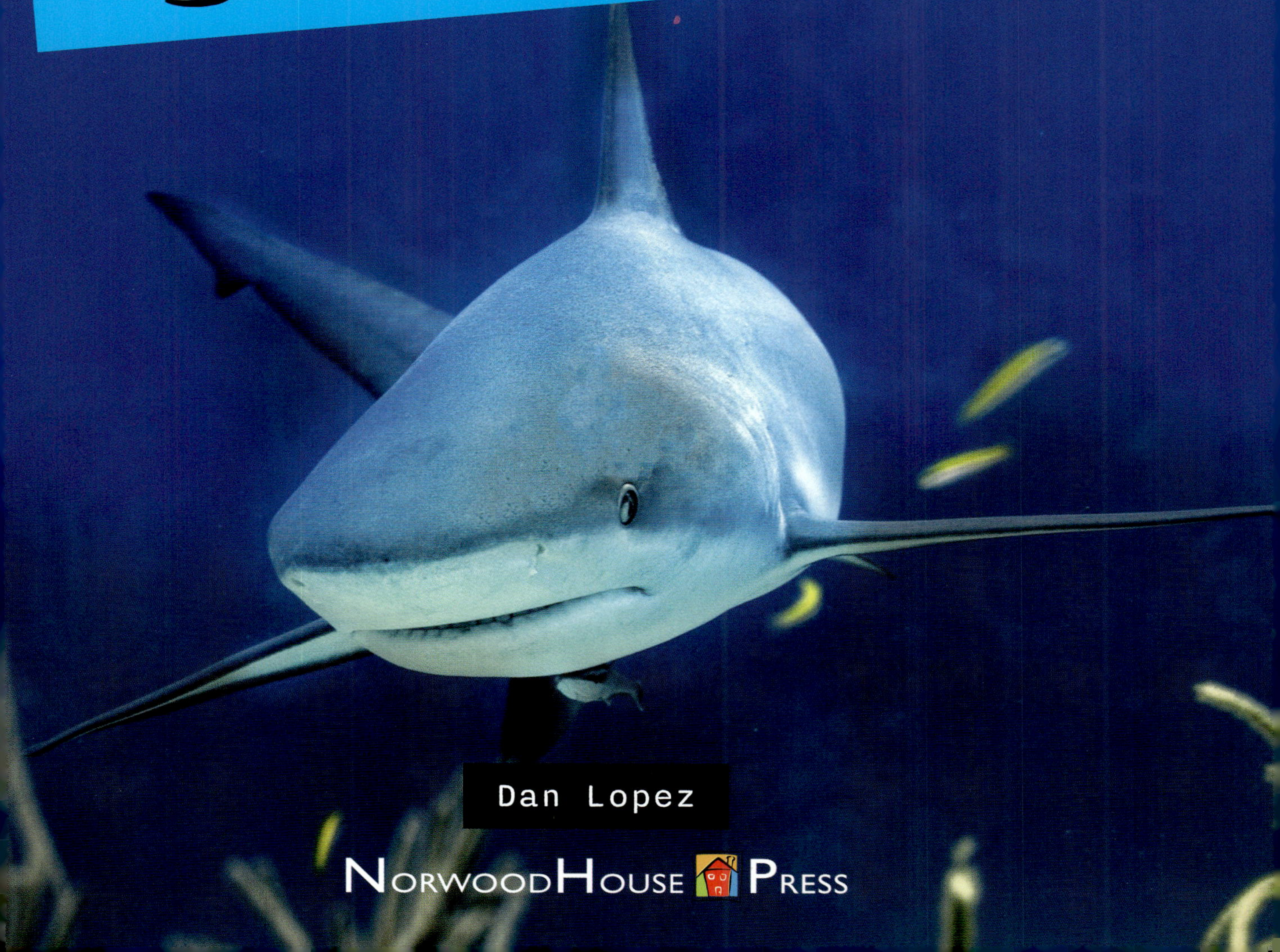

Dan Lopez

NorwoodHouse Press

Cataloging-in-Publication Data

Names: Lopez, Dan.
Title: Bull shark / Dan Lopez.
Description: Buffalo, NY : Norwood House Press, 2027. | Series: Super sharks | Includes glossary and index.
Identifiers: ISBN 9781978581432 (pbk.) | ISBN 9781978581449 (library bound) | ISBN 9781978581456 (ebook)
Subjects: LCSH: Bull shark--Juvenile literature.
Classification: LCC QL638.95.C3 L67 2027 | DDC 597.34--dc23

Published in 2027 by
Norwood House Press
2544 Clinton Street
Buffalo, NY 14224

Copyright © 2027 Norwood House Press
Designer: Rhea Magaro
Editor: Tricia Hoffman

Photo credits: Cover, p. 1 Wirestock Creators/Shutterstock.com; p. 5 msriddleabroad/Shutterstock.com; p. 6 Tomas Kotouc/Shutterstock.com; p. 9 Jose Angel Astor Rocha/Shutterstock.com; p. 10 Wirestock Creators/Shutterstock.com; p. 11 Stefan Pircher/Shutterstock.com; p. 12 Captainess_travels/Shutterstock.com; p. 15 FOODIES ACADEMY/Shutterstock.com; p. 16 Aquarius Traveller/Shutterstock.com; p. 19 chatchai kusolsinchai/Shutterstock.com; p. 21 Shawn murphy media/Shutterstock.com;

All rights reserved. No part of this book may be reproduced in any form without permission in writing from the publisher, except by a reviewer.

Printed in the United States of America

Some of the images in this book illustrate individuals who are models. The depictions do not imply actual situations or events.

CPSIA compliance information: Batch #CSNHP27: For further information contact Norwood House Press at 1-800-237-9932.

Find us on

TABLE OF CONTENTS

What Is Special about Bull Sharks? 4
What Do Bull Sharks Look Like? 6
Where Do Bull Sharks Live? 13
How Do Bull Sharks Hunt? 14
How Do Bull Sharks Reproduce? 20
Glossary 22
Thinking Questions 23
Index 24
About the Author 24

What Is Special about Bull Sharks?

Bull sharks are one of the only kinds of shark that can live in fresh water. They swim up **coastal** rivers. They have been found thousands of miles away from the ocean!

Of all sharks, bull sharks are one of the most likely to attack humans.

What Do Bull Sharks Look Like?

Compared to its length, a bull shark is wide. This makes it look **stout** and sturdy, like a bull!

These sharks can be 13 feet (four meters) long. They can weigh 700 pounds (320 kilograms).

The top of a bull shark's body is gray. The belly is white. This provides **camouflage**. Seen from above, the shark blends in with the water. Seen from below, it blends in with the sunlight.

The bull shark has long **pectoral fins**. Its front **dorsal fin** is a large, pointed triangle. The back dorsal fin is much smaller.

This big fish has tiny eyes. It does not see well.

Where Do Bull Sharks Live?

Bull sharks are found in oceans, **estuaries**, and coastal rivers all over the world. They usually swim in shallow water near shorelines and beaches.

How Do Bull Sharks Hunt?

Bull sharks hunt alone. When searching for food, they can be **aggressive**.

They are capable of short bursts of speed. An attacking bull shark can swim up to 25 miles (40 kilometers) per hour.

Bull sharks are not picky eaters. They hunt for fish, stingrays, dolphins, and other sharks. Sometimes, they catch a seabird or a turtle. They have even been known to eat dogs!

Like charging bulls, bull sharks **headbutt** their **prey**. This stuns the animal. Then, the shark attacks with big, **serrated** teeth. This hunting method is sometimes called "bump and bite."

How Do Bull Sharks Reproduce?

Females have their babies in warm, shallow, protected waters. They give birth to live babies, or pups. Up to 13 can be born at one time.

GLOSSARY

aggressive (uh-GRES-iv): threatening; ready to attack

camouflage (KAM-uh-flahzh): a disguise or natural coloring that lets animals hide by making them look like their surroundings

coastal (KOH-stuhl): near the ocean

dorsal fin (DOR-sl fin): a flat, thin body part that sticks up from the back of a shark or other marine animal

estuaries (ES-choo-er-eez): wide areas where rivers meet the ocean; estuaries are important habitats where many ocean animals raise their young

headbutt (HED-but): to hit with the head

pectoral fins (PEK-tuh-ruhl finz): fins on both sides of an aquatic animal that act like arms to guide the animal through water

prey (pray): animals eaten by other animals

serrated (SER-ay-tid): notched like the blade of a saw

stout (stout): large, strong, and heavily built; fat

Thinking Questions

1. How is a bull shark like a bull?
2. How are bull sharks different from other sharks?
3. Give one reason that bull sharks are dangerous to people.
4. What do bull sharks eat?
5. How do bull sharks catch prey?

Index

colors 8

fins 10

food 14, 17

fresh water 4

people 4

pups 20

rivers 4, 13

size 6

speed 14

teeth 18

About the Author

Dan Lopez lives far from the ocean in Indianapolis, Indiana, with his wife and three kids. He is fascinated by all of Earth's animals, including sharks! He admires their sleekness and speed and thinks more people should appreciate them.